Meatatarian:

The Next Level of the Paleo Diet

Maggie B. Conklin, B.A., ND

Edited by Rebecca Haack

Book layout by Rebecca Haack

Charcuterie designed by Michael Bild

Photography by Christine Ferris

This book is intended to provide educational information for the reader on the covered subject. It is not intended to take the place of personalized medical counseling, diagnosis, and treatment from a trained health professional.

© 2018 by Maggie B. Conklin

All rights reserved. No part of this book may be reproduced without written permission from the author, except by a reviewer who may quote brief passages in a review with appropriate credits; nor may any part of this book be reproduced, stored in a retrieval system, or transmitted in any form or by any means – electronic, mechanical, photocopying, recording, or other – without written permission from the author.

ISBN: 9781976919206

Printed in the United States by Kindle Direct Publishing

10 9 8 7 6 5 4 3 2 1

Dedicated to my darling, ever so patient, and long-suffering husband, Ron.

Table of Contents

Introduction 1

Chapter 1: Many Reasons (Excuses) to be Vegetarian 5

Chapter 2: A Big Clue That We're Meant to Eat Meat 15

Chapter 3: Essential Nutrients 23

Chapter 4: The Paleo Short Story 31

Chapter 5: Taking Paleo to the Next Level 39

Chapter 6: How to Eat Like Your Ancestors 47

Chapter 7: What to Drink 63

Chapter 8: Frequently Asked Questions 71

Chapter 9: Moderation, My Friends 85

Chapter 10: Find Your Meatatarian Way 91

References 95

Foreword

When I was first asked to read this book and write an introduction, I wasn't really sure what I was going to be reading. I wondered what a meatatarian was and just how it related to the average person.

As soon as I read the first few paragraphs, I said, "Oh, this is going to be pretty useful to me and my practice as an herbalist and naturopath." I realized within the first few paragraphs that this was just the sort of book I needed as a handy reference tool when interacting with clients who had qualms about meat and the ways in which they could incorporate it within their diet.

In the Deep South, we have always had a love affair with our cast iron skillets, many of which are often passed down from generation to generation. As anyone who uses cast iron knows, before using it, it is critical that it be properly seasoned in order to avoid getting food stuck. Reading further on in *Meatatarian*, I saw where this was exactly what Maggie was so clearly explaining. WE are seasoned to the land and environment where we and our ancestors originated. We developed a desire and tolerance for the foods our hunter/gatherer ancestors ate on a daily basis.

One of the things I appreciate about *Meatatarian* is that the concept of eating as our ancestors did is so clearly addressed, as are potential meals and food combinations. While this doesn't mean we can't eat other foods, it does let the reader know that for optimal health, eating as we were "seasoned" is the way to go.

Another concept addressed is how readers can get the vitamins and minerals from their diet to compensate for their food choices. If the reader is a die-hard vegetarian, there are options to aid in rounding out the diet when meat simply is not an option.

Education, recipes, and a clear explanation of why meat is actually an essential element of a healthy diet make this book an invaluable addition to any bookshelf. By following the guidelines in this book, the reader will find it much easier to lead a balanced and healthy quality of life while avoiding doctor visits.

Darryl Patton, M.A., ND

Introduction

I am a naturopath practicing in Michigan. Please understand that most of the general public in the Great State of Michigan have never heard of a naturopath, and in case you haven't either, I'll sum it up for you: Naturopaths are healers who practice natural health care. We do not prescribe. We always try to find the cause of a disease and, by addressing the cause, assist clients in taking away that cause so that their bodies can heal.

Pretty cool, huh?

We can use many different modalities, including special diets, exercise, supplements, herbs, teas, tinctures, homeopathic remedies, massage therapy, chiropractic therapy, applied kinesiology, acupressure, acupuncture, and any number of other specialties. We find out quickly after starting our practices that *every single body is very different, and no one diet is right for everyone.* Please read that last line again because it's important. Keep this knowledge in mind while reading this book and any other book, article, or report about diet and health.

I've written this book because so many people come into my office and assume that I'm a vegetarian. Because a vegetarian diet is healthy, right? Wrong. Very wrong.

It's almost impossible to get the nutrients we need from non-animal sourced foods and drinks. We, as humans, must have vitamin B_{12} in our diets. This family of vitamins is called cobalamins and includes the two most widely recognized: cyanocobalamin and methocobalamin. Vitamin B_{12} is a whole family of vitamins, and vegetarians are often told that the herb comfrey is a source of this necessary vitamin. But here's the catch: you almost have to overdose on comfrey tea to get enough.

And besides, who wants to sit around all day drinking cup after cup of bland tea?

Vitamin B_{12} is available aplenty in meat protein. Just sayin'.

We'll go into more deficiencies later, but this one is easy and has dozens of clinical trials and science-y stuff behind it. Why would you think that being a vegetarian or vegan was healthy, or even natural, if you are forced to take a synthetic vitamin to make up for it?

Chapter 1
Many Reasons (Excuses) to be Vegetarian

As a naturopath, I see many people who are vegetarian at my store and in consultation. They're usually surprised when they find out that I'm not a vegetarian, and I read their expressions in different ways. Sometimes they look at me with surprise, as if they are shocked. Sometimes disappointment appears on their faces. Oftentimes I can't pretend to understand their expressions.

I used to feel like I should apologize for not being vegetarian, but quickly figured out that was the wrong attitude. Then I tried to educate them about the dangers of vegetarianism and (gasp!) vegan-ism. Finally

I decided to write this book and free myself and the rest of us "normal" humans from the guilt of being a meatatarian.

Viva Meatatarians!

When I've asked clients why they are vegetarian or vegan I've gotten as many answers as people, but I put most of them into one of five categories:

1. Because of my faith.
2. Because that's how my parents raised me.
3. Because I feel sorry for the animals.
4. Because it's not sustainable.
5. Because it's healthy.

Let's work these answers in order.

If someone tells me that they are on a special vegetarian or vegan diet **because of their faith**, well then, I'll let them be. That's the trump card and I won't try to talk them out of it. What I will do, however, is take the time to educate them on which supplements they must take to prevent long-term body structural damage and to prevent some very specific nutritional malnourishments.

"That's how my parents raised me" doesn't happen very often, but when it does, it's magic. I then ask them if their parents had health problems later in life, and my first guess is usually diabetes or Alzheimer's disease. You see, a vegetarian diet is inherently very high in carbohydrates (sugars) and low in proteins, so anyone who is genetically predisposed to blood sugar problems will often become hypoglycemic or diabetic after a decade or two as a vegetarian. I also ask if their parents had joint problems, especially with bad hips or knees where the cartilage wore out. Eating meats cooked with the bones in, eating the cartilage and bone marrow, gelatin, and collagen, can certainly prevent or at least slow down joint problems like these.

You might already know about taking the supplement glucosamine, usually combined with chondroitin, for healthy joints. Well, did you know that glucosamine is made from beef, pork, chicken, or shark cartilage? Did you know that chondroitin is made from shrimp shells, essentially the exoskeleton of shrimp?

Yes, I've also met a number of people who "cured" their diabetes after becoming vegetarian, but I rack that up to the fact that they 1) are eating a lot less foods in quantity, and 2) have become aware of the dangers of "bad" foods and "junk foods" in general and have taken them out of their daily diets. You can easily see how taking out sweet snacks and junk foods and replacing them with fresh fruits and vegetables will help a diabetic. It's a great "ah-ha" moment and I applaud them for it! But after a year or three it's time to introduce some good animal proteins into their diets again.

I have a long-time family friend who became vegetarian when she was around 20 years old. When I asked her "Why?" she said that she did it to stay thin. Of course, any prohibitive diet would have worked, but vegetarians can eat lots of tasty carbohydrates and still stay thin, so that's what she did. Fast-forward 20 years and she's still fairly healthy, but struggles with her weight daily. I don't wonder what happened. About once a year I asked her to at least add eggs to her diet, so finally she went all-in and bought hens and built a chicken coop. You go, girl! I saw her a few months later and she'd slimmed right down.

The first time I met someone who was vegetarian "because that's how her parents raised her" we were in Alaska fishing for salmon. She was a talented fisherman and caught her limit of fish on the first day, but she wouldn't eat the fish. That's what started the discussion.

Me: "So you're a vegetarian, but apparently you don't mind catching fish and other people eating them. And salmon is arguably one of the healthiest things to eat. I don't get it."

Her: "Well, that's how my parents raised us. We eat very healthy, but we don't eat meat."

Me: "Hm."

Her: "Hm!"

Oh, the look on her face! A couple years later we met again and although she called herself a vegetarian, she was now an ovo lacto vegetarian that also ate fish. (People who are vegetarians but still eat eggs, yogurt, and cheese are called "ovo lacto vegetarians.")

Me: "Score!"

This brings us to the animal lovers. When my dear, sweet, vegan niece was trying to get pregnant and simply couldn't conceive I had a gentle discussion with her. Actually it was a bunch of short discussions over a three-day, two-night visit. In my normal way, after I listened to her lament about not conceiving I asked her why she was vegan. She said, "Because I can't bring myself to eat anything from an animal. And, **I feel so sorry for the farmed animals** and the terrible way they are treated."

Pout. Big, blue, sad, watery eyes.

I gave that to her for the day, hoping she connected my question to her concern about conception. Then the next day I snuck in little pearls of wisdom about how vegans can't possibly get enough vitamin B_{12} as well as other essential nutrients. Her answer was that she used to take some vitamin B_{12} but it ran out and she never bought it again. "Perhaps you should, along with a good strong B-complex vitamin. It couldn't hurt, right?" I nudged.

Later that day I asked her, "Does your doctor think you're anemic?" She looked at me with surprise and confirmed that to be true. "Well, although there are vegetable sources of iron," I explained, "it's not the kind of iron our bodies need. We need 'heme iron,' which is only found in animal-sourced protein." She said she'd get an iron supplement.

The morning before we left to go home I snuck in the last suggestion: "What if I told you that I think you might be too malnourished to get pregnant, and that eating four or five eggs a week and two servings of salmon would probably be enough to get pregnant. Would you do it?"

She looked thoughtful for a moment and answered yes, she could source local farm raised free-range unfertilized chicken eggs and convince herself to eat them "for the sake of the child." I then wondered out loud if she could perhaps add two whole servings of salmon a week to her diet. Yes, she seemed to answer herself, if she could find wild caught Pacific Alaskan yadda-yadda-yadda salmon she could choke that down twice a week.

Two months later she conceived.

I visited her again a couple of years ago to find that she had "fallen off the vegan wagon" and was eating meat with every meal. My sweet niece pleaded with me, "Why am I craving meat all the time? I've been eating it for months now and I still can't get enough." My answer was that she had been vegan for years, and it would take more than a couple of months to recover. She said she was up for the challenge as she munched down a strip of bacon.

Once in a great while I find myself talking with someone who is vegetarian because, according to them, "eating meat is not sustainable." Does that mean the world will end and children will starve if we aren't all vegetarians? No. Children are starving today, right down the road from where you live, whether you want to believe it or not. The fact of the matter is that here in the good old U. S. of A. we throw away more than a third, yes, 33%, of the food that we bring home from the grocery store. Once we figure out how to teach people to only buy what they're going to eat in the next couple of days, as well as other tips on preventing spoilage, then we can fix the sustainability problem. Personally, I don't really see how vegetarianism affects sustainability, but that's probably fodder for another book.

So many people walk into my shop and proudly announce that **they are vegetarian or vegan "because it's so healthy."** They assume they've walked into a place that "gets them" and their way of life. Frankly, they look like they've been vegetarian for a long time. Their hair is limp, thin, and colorless. Their faces have soft wrinkles and their jowls sag. Their lips have a blue tint because of long-term iron deficiency. The skin on their arms and legs sag. Their muscle tone is lacking. They are wearing Birkenstock shoes (sigh).

Honestly, I usually don't even try to educate them on more than the obvious reasons I'm a meatatarian. One sentence to them, maybe two, before I offer them some B_{12} and a non-constipating form of iron.

Veganism is not a healthy long-term diet. Short-term, alright, but not long-term. Contrarily, the Atkin's Diet and other high protein extremely low carbohydrate diets aren't necessarily healthy either, as most of them allow plenty of factory made processed foods so the author/company can make money on those foods and the dieters/purchasers can continue to have a convenient diet. Dr. Atkin passed away while walking down the sidewalk in front of his home. They didn't do an autopsy but it was rumored "in the industry" that he had an aneurism or stroke. But I guess we all have to die of something.

The point I'm trying to make goes back to the third paragraph of this book: "We find out quickly after starting our practices that every single body is very different, and no one diet is right for everyone." In this book you and I will travel around the world together to find the best diet for your body. Let's get going.

Chapter 2
A Big Clue That We're Meant to Eat Meat

Mammals are animals that nurse their young. They have mammary glands; we call them "breasts" on humans. And they come in three groups of eaters: carnivores, vegetarians, and omnivores. Carnivores get their nutrition primarily by eating other animals, with some vegetable matter to round out the diet. Vegetarians get their nutrition primarily from plants, and they usually eat a few bugs while they're doing it, so they do get some protein along with the plants.

Omnivores eat both plants and animals, and need both to get their necessary nutrients.

Carnivores include the canine family of wolves, coyotes, and dingoes; the feline family of cougars, lions, mongooses, and hyenas (yes, hyenas are genetically closer to cats than dogs); sea mammals such as orca and porpoise; and raptors, including eagles, hawks, owls, and falcons. Oh, and woodpeckers. Okay, I know that birds aren't mammals but I love them, and I'm writing this, so I've taken the artistic license to include them.

Vegetarian (herbivore) mammals include antelope, cows, dear, elk, and moose as well as sheep, rabbits, squirrels, chipmunks, and other rodents. The bovine (cow) family of mammals has two or more stomachs or other highly modified digestion systems to assist in breaking down and assimilating all of that high fiber vegetable matter.

Humans don't have such a highly efficient digestive system, do they? They also don't have the types of digestive enzymes needed to assimilate high quantities of fibrous vegetable matter and legumes (beans).

Omnivore mammals include pigs, bears, hedgehogs, and raccoons, as well as birds such as chickens, ducks, and songbirds like robins and cardinals. And yes, humans. Omnivores need nutrients from animals and plants to grow to a healthy, ripe old age. Most birds eat a lot of seeds and at least a few insects too, which are mostly protein and chitin ("kite-in"), the stuff that the exoskeleton of insects and shrimp are made of.

Take a look at these herbivores/vegetarians:

Now take a look at some omnivores/carnivores:

What similarities do you notice between the herbivores and omnivores? Do you notice any differences between the herbivores and omnivores and these carnivores?

Notice the one big difference between vegetarians and omnivores/carnivores? Vegetarian's eyes are almost always on the sides of their heads. Carnivore's eyes are almost always on the front of their heads. Omnivore's eyes are usually on the front of their heads, but not always.

Where are your eyes?

Next question: What do your teeth look like?

The front teeth (incisors) of herbivores are made to cut and bite, gnaw and scrape vegetable matter. They do not have canine teeth, and their molars and premolars (teeth on the side used for chewing) have flat, grinding surfaces that keep growing throughout their lives. I learned this the hard way when my family had horses and the veterinarian had to file down my horse Linda's molars once every year or two because they weren't lined up right and didn't grind down properly. Gnawing herbivores do not have canine teeth, while ruminant herbivores do have canines that look and act more like incisors than canines.

The front teeth (incisors) of carnivores are more pointed so that they can hold on to the prey that they catch. Their molars and premolars are more uneven and they do not keep growing throughout their lives.

Humans have similar incisors, molars, and premolars as carnivores. Humans also have canine teeth, although it's arguable that they are a hybrid of incisors and the longer canines of the feline and canine families. I'll give you that.

Think about the animals that we humans are most closely related to. There's some argument here, but DNA testing is helpful. Yes, you probably thought about apes, chimpanzees, and monkeys, right? Recent science has humans more closely related to pigs, so when a nice, young woman says something like, "I had a date last night, but he turned out to be such a pig!" she might not be kidding. But in all seriousness, I have often wondered if this fact is why some ethnicities – notably Jewish, Muslim, and some Hindu practitioners – refrain from pork.

It's OK if you don't eat pork, or any other specific food source or type, because there are so many other great things to eat. Even though I offer menu ideas from specific world regions in Chapter 6, please always try to broaden your food horizon by sampling healthful fresh and seasonal foods from all regions of the world on occasion.

Chapter 3
Essential Nutrients

My apologies if this part is too science-y and a bit boring, but it might be the most important factor in understanding why we need to eat meat.

Amino acids are long-chain proteins that are most easily sourced from – you guessed it – animal meat. The food supplement L-taurine is made by a purely synthetic process using sodium bisulfite, liquid ammonia, sulfuric acid, and purified water. But other amino acids are made from more down-to-earth things.

There is a very popular amino acid in the body building and sports nutrition industry called N-acetyl-L-cysteine. It's made from either duck feathers (likely from ducks that ended up as a delectable Chinese Crispy Duck dish) or (this even makes me gag) human hair. I've been told the hair is purchased from prison camps, but I can't prove that.

Ew. Just ew.

I'll get my aminos from steak, roasts, eggs, and bacon, thankyouverymuch. It's so much more appetizing that way.

So what do amino acids do for humans? In plain language, every cell of your body is constantly breaking down and rebuilding itself. Your spleen, for instance, takes your red blood cells and looks at each one as it circulates through. If a particular red blood cell isn't healthy, or is damaged, the spleen completely breaks it down and either throws it away through the bowels or rebuilds it using spare parts. Yes, it uses the parts of broken down red blood cells to build new ones! It also uses the building blocks of red blood cells, mostly different amino acids, to rebuild them. And where do those amino acids come from? You guessed it: most easily from animal protein.

Thus it follows that people who don't have enough animal protein in their diet might have poor or deficient red blood cells. People with low red blood cell counts may be prone to a weak immune system, and more colds, flu, and allergies than meatatarians.

It also follows logically that vegetarians and vegans are anemic, or low in iron. Many of them think they can eat vegetables that are high in iron like kelp and molasses, or seeds and nuts, but that's not the case. There are two types of iron: heme and non-heme. "Heme" is Latin for "blood" and heme iron is necessary for the spleen to work efficiently. Non-heme iron, from non-animals, isn't digested as well in human stomachs, isn't as easily assimilated into the body, and doesn't assist the spleen in repairing red blood cells. Not very well, at least.

So, people who don't eat enough quality animal protein often have a spleen in poor health.

Do you like saggy cheeks? Lots of wrinkles and laugh lines? Thin, brittle fingernails and unhealthy toe nails? Dull, limp, colorless hair? Do you want "bat wings" (you know, when the under part of your biceps sag and waddle)? Then become a vegan. Animal protein is the building block for repairing your muscles, skin, hair, and nails. That's why so many bottles of gelatin and other collagen products are sold in health food stores every year.

Dr. Elson Haas, M.D., describes the symptoms of iron anemia in his book *Staying Healthy with Nutrition.* He says, "Fatigue and lack of stamina usually arise first, caused by fewer red blood cells, low hemoglobin, and a reduced ability to hold and carry oxygen. Children who are iron deficient may experience psychological problems, learning disabilities based on hyper-activity or a decreased attention span, and even a lower IQ, besides other symptoms of anemia. Headaches, dizziness, weight loss from decreased appetite, constipation, and lowered immunity may occur. With anemia, paleness of the skin, cheeks, lips, and tongue may occur, as can a sore tongue, canker sores in the mouth, hair loss, itching, and brittle nails. Not uncommon is a general state of apathy, irritability, and/or depression – a lack of enthusiasm for life – which can, however, improve rapidly with iron supplementation. Decreased memory may also occur. In children particularly, iron deficiency may cause a strange symptom called "pica" – eating and sucking on inedible objects, such as toys, clay, or ice."

    Do you and your loved ones want to have beautiful tight skin, with few wrinkles, firm muscle tone, healthy finger and toe nails, and beautiful, long, buoyant hair that's rich in color? Then put a roast in the crock pot or a bunch of shrimp on the bar-b-que. It's the least you can do to prevent coming home and finding your vegan loved-one sucking on the furniture.

And here's a really important trick that you should use: cook meat with the bones *in*. Put a whole beef, pork or lamb roast in the oven or the crock pot, bones and all. Cook fish with the bones in, or eat sardines, which are offered that way. Cook seafood in the shells, roast turkey and fowl whole, grill a T-bone or porterhouse steak. There are nutrients in the bones and shells that we need to rebuild the structures of our human bodies. Not only are bones dense with minerals like calcium, magnesium, potassium, phosphorus, and many others, but the marrow has nutrients that are necessary for our immune system. Homemade chicken noodle soup anyone?

Bones are high in proteins, including collagen and gelatin, both of which are needed to repair connective tissues like ligaments and tendons. If you're a runner or athlete, I believe you need even more of these forms of protein to keep your tendons healthy, prevent your ligaments from snapping, and replace and rebuild the cartilage cushioning all of your joints. We know from hundreds of clinical trials that glucosamine and chondroitin alleviate joint pain and prevent cartilage degradation, right? Well, what are they made of?

Glucosamine is most commonly made from bovine, chicken, or shark cartilage, and chondroitin is most commonly manufactured out of shrimp shells. You are what you eat.

We mentioned vitamin B_{12} in Chapter 1 and this deficiency creates even more symptoms than we discussed earlier. According to Dr. Haas: "With B_{12} deficiency, the body forms large, immature red blood cells, resulting in a 'megaloblastic' anemia… This anemia usually generates more fatigue and weakness. Menstrual problems, even amenorrhea (lack of menstrual flow) may also occur in B_{12}-deficient women."

Dr. Haas goes on to explain how this type of anemia can cause nervous system damage, possibly permanent, as well as brain and spinal cord damage, which can lead to nerve pain, numbness, weakened muscles, shooting pains, and even hallucinations and paranoia. A sure sign of B_{12}-deficiency is a red, sore, even ulcerated tongue.

How are we supposed to enjoy our food with a red, sore, ulcerated tongue?

So if, after finishing this book (all of it, to the end), you decide that you still are happier as a vegetarian/vegan, then please let me list some supplements that have clinical evidence toward supporting this lifestyle and diet. And guys? Keep taking them, for as long as you're on that diet.

1. Vitamin B_{12}, preferably in the methylcobalamin form, which works better than the cyanocobalamin form.
2. A good, strong B-complex vitamin. I suggest at least 50 mgs/mcs of each, and preferable a B-75 or B-100.
3. A non-constipating form of iron, like iron (ferrous) glycinate.
4. Amino acid blend capsules with all of the essential aminos included.

Chapter 4
The Paleo Short Story

I was blessed with a great childhood. My father was a hunter and fisherman, my mother was a gourmet, and we ate a generally Paleo diet every day. And this was back in the '60s, '70s, and '80s, way before "Paleo" was cool.

My father would bring home elk, caribou, moose, and bighorn sheep. Southern fish including yellowtail tuna and grouper, and crayfish when they were in season. Alaskan seafood like halibut, four different kinds of salmon, and fresh ocean-harvested shrimp. And oh! The

Dungeness crab! Also fresh fish from Lake Michigan, a few miles from where we lived. In autumn he'd bring home fowl including goose, pheasant, and many types of ducks.

Mother had dozens of ways to prepare the bounty so we would never get tired of the dinners. She had close to a hundred cookbooks from around the world. Her favorite recipes were marked with an old school project, a letter from a friend, or a photograph from a vacation. She especially loved French cooking and adored Julia Child. Her sauces were "to die for."

We ate a largely Paleo diet. What's that, you ask? The short answer is that a Paleo diet is abundant in fresh foods similar to what cavemen ate, or more specifically, your distant ancestors. Modern highly processed foods are devoid of nutrients. Even our fresh fruits and vegetables are noticeably lower in nutrients than they used to be because they are grown in overworked soils. So if we can go back to eating the way our ancestors ate, then we'll eat a more highly nutritious diet, right?

Consider wheat flour. Wheat is largely grown in soil that's been farmed for well over a hundred years. The farmers have to apply artificial plant food just to get the crops to grow. Some of these fertilizers are more expensive than seaweed (also known as kelp) which is a fabulous plant food but underutilized and virtually unknown to the modern factory farmer. They then harvest the wheat and let it sit in hot, humid silos for weeks or months before sending it to a mill. Once it's milled it is more likely to become rancid, so they bleach it, effectively neutralizing any residual nutrients that might be left. Oxidation is also in action here, depleting the nutritional value of milled grains within days.

Store-bought flour is so completely devoid of nutrients that the U.S. Government makes the flour mills and flour companies add five vitamins (synthetic vitamins) back into the flour because they noticed that people who had diets high in wheat flour became malnourished.

However, grow wheat or any other grain in fresh, rich soil, harvest it, and mill it right before using it in whatever delicious meal you had in mind, and it is quite healthful. But that's a lot of work and just not possible for most of us – myself included.

So what might a typical day of Paleo food look like for me?

Breakfast
Egg omelet with goat cheese and some kind of green, like spinach, watercress, or fennel.

Mid-morning snack (if needed)
A handful of fresh, seasonally ripe fruit, like berries, nuts, or an apple or pear.

Lunch
Leek potato soup with a side of leftover meat from last night.

Mid-afternoon snack (if needed)
Herbal tea, locally harvested. My favorites are sassafras, staghorn sumac fruit "lemonade," or anything in the mint family like spearmint, catnip, oregano, or motherwort.

Dinner

Fresh catch of the day poached in wine and butter, served on sautéed onions and mushrooms. Serve with craft beer, perhaps a kolsch or saison.

Eating a Paleo diet in my household is based on a lifetime of stocking and making fresh food. The rest of this chapter is dedicated to sharing what I do; you may want to adopt some of these practices yourself.

First, we home brew beer and make our wine, either from a wine kit or from wild grapes. A really nice five-gallon wine kit ends up being between $2.00 and $5.00 a bottle and makes more than 30 bottles. (Understand that this part has taken years of practice and work to learn, with the help of my husband.)

A full-size freezer sits in our garage filled with wild-caught fish, fowl, and game. About once a year, we also split a grass-fed cow with friends. I make sure to get the healthiest bits: liver, kidneys, tongue (lingua), and "sweetbread," which is actually the thymus gland of the cow, not the brain. Yes, this is expensive and takes some finagling. However, we end up with a quarter of a cow with all of the different cuts of beef, hamburger, and breakfast sausage, all for close to the same price as plain hamburger in the local grocery store. I'd say that's worth it. The hardest thing to do once you have a fully stocked freezer is to remember to take the meat out to thaw.

    Our pantry always has certain staples that find their way into most every meal. This includes brown rice, wild rice, and a few bags of hard beans like black eyed peas, black beans, and split peas. Potatoes and onions are always on hand. Plus, we keep a ready supply of Irish or steel cut oatmeal, flax seeds, and other seeds and nuts (preferably raw and unsalted and still in their shells).

    Also, I do a lot of canning of meats and vegetables. I can't live without canned tomatoes, and I don't want to live without canned beets, both plain and pickled. Green beans and asparagus round out my pantry. Of course, cave men didn't use a pressure cooker, and we humans have only been canning since the mid-1800s, but it's worth it to me.

Really, with a well-stocked pantry and freezer you can whip up just about any dinner with very little notice.

See how simple it is? You could have bought any number of books that drone on and on about Paleo diets and eating, and you got it right here in just a few short pages! You're welcome.

Chapter 5
Taking Paleo to The Next Level

Okay, so eating a Paleo diet means eating like a caveman. You got that, right? Let's take it to the next level now.

Eat like your ancestors.

Your ancestors, not anyone else's ancestors.

The American Journal of Clinical Nutrition published peer-reviewed clinical information in March of 2000 on plant versus animal ratios in the diets of the few remaining indigenous (hunter-gatherer) societies of the world. Many people were surprised by the report, which stated that of these peoples 73% of them derived more than 50% of their calories from animal sourced foods. Fourteen percent of them obtained less than 50% of their daily calories from animal sourced foods. The study went on to say that as the climate became colder, plant consumption decreased while fish consumption increased.

What does this mean for you? Well, if your ancestors came from the equatorial regions of the world like Central America, the Mediterranean, India, South East Asia, and the Polynesian Islands, then your most healthful diet might consist of a variety of wild grown vegetables, fresh fruits, and some grains, and between 25% and 45% animal proteins and fats. If your ancestors lived closer to the polar regions of the world including Siberia, Canada, Mongolia, and Southern Argentina and Peru, then at least 50% of the calories in your daily diet could come from cold water fish like halibut, cod, salmon, and herring. Include some antlered animals like elk and moose to round out the protein, and the balance of your diet could consist of wild grains, root vegetables, greens, and berries.

If your ancestors came from someplace in between the poles and the equator, closer to the Tropic of Capricorn or Cancer, let's figure a protein to plant material ratio somewhere between these two extremes for your ideal diet.

So if your ancestors were from the **Mediterranean** area (Italy, Spain, Greece, Egypt, and all of the countries surrounding the Mediterranean Sea), then your body probably does very well eating a diet rich in seafood, lamb, olive oil, lots of herbs and spices, and nightshade vegetables like tomatoes, eggplant, potatoes, and okra.

If your family line came from **Northern Europe** (including England, the Netherlands, Eastern Russia, and the Scandinavian countries), then I suspect that your body thrives on cold water fish like cod and halibut, Old World grains like barley and oats, greens in the spring and summer only, and root vegetables like carrots, parsnips, and rutabagas in the winter. Oh! And squash… lots of squash.

South-East Asians (those whose family is from Thailand, Vietnam, Laos, Cambodia, Malaysia, Indonesia and the Philippines) are most likely to be able to be healthy on a highly vegetarian diet because these countries historically eat the least amount of animal matter. These folks eat a lot of brown rice and red rice, actually quite a few different types of rice. Of course, they are not eating white rice that is de-hulled mechanically and thus deprived of its nutrients. For meat they eat mostly seafood, including squid and mollusks if they live near water and mainly pork or fowl if they live inland. This area of the world is rich in forests and plants and the people have eaten a wide variety of fruits and vegetables throughout history. Don't forget that spices and herbs should be present in each meal.

Native Central and South Americans have an entire continent covered in rich vegetation and a culture steeped in thousands of years of cultivating crops and livestock, forests filled with edible and medicinal plants, wildlife, and beautiful coastlines of oceans, inland lakes, and rivers filled with seafood. Nobody should go hungry in South America. We are looking at perhaps the most well rounded diet in the world, with cultivated legumes, corn, and grains, wild and raised animals, fresh bush and tree fruits, nuts, fish, squid, wild boar, and goats and sheep. We are blessed to be able to see so many of the peoples of South America still living as their ancestors lived. Some may consider them destitute, but I consider them rich in so many ways.

Native North Americans including the far north "First Tribes" of the Inuit and Eskimo might have the diet highest in animal protein and fat in the world. Around the globe, the people of the far north must eat enormous amounts of fat to survive extreme temperatures, long winters, and long summer days of hunting and gathering. They have very little vegetable matter, but do eat a lot of fruits in season. Those who eat this specialized diet, like their ancestors, rarely have diabetes, tooth decay, or even high cholesterol. Imagine that! Eating large quantities of animal fat and whale lard and having balanced cholesterol levels. We can assume a similar diet for those peoples from Siberia and most of the northern parts of Russia and China.

The Native Americans of the more southerly United States also historically ate a diet high in meat and fat, with fruits and vegetables grown and gathered seasonally. Corn, squash, and many different kinds of legumes are written about, but there isn't much use of spices as we think of them today. Since there are many types of wild onions in North America, let's presume they used those for flavor, as well as the hundreds of herbs that we know they used for cooking and medicinal teas.

The Middle East is rich in so many cultural histories and is another area like South America where some of the peoples still largely live like their ancestors did a thousand years ago. Many of these people still raise livestock, grow small family gardens, travel and trade with their neighbors near and far, and cook almost every meal at home. Because the Middle East is literally the crossroads between Africa, Asia, Europe, and Russia they have pulled the best of the best of the foods, spices, and herbs from all of the surrounding areas and made their own wonderful, succulent cuisine.

Africa is a large continent with many different regions and it may be difficult to know which area your ancestors are from, especially if your family has been off that fine continent for many generations. The northernmost points of Africa include the Mediterranean countries that we touched on earlier. Moving south, we go into the Sahara Desert with its caravans of roving tribes, eating very little locally. In comparison, the western shores of Africa are rich with wildlife, rain forests filled with bountiful vegetation, uncountable variations of fruits and vegetables, and the Atlantic Ocean teaming with seafood. The western and southern portions of Africa have been cultivating crops for thousands of years and their diets are rich in root vegetables (especially plants in the yam family), some grains, and tree fruits, as well as antelope and small game. Again, they work hard for their protein and don't waste any portion of the animal, considering organ meat like the heart, liver, and other organs as prized portions of the meal.

So where are your ancestors from? I realize that today most people have some mixed heritage, whether they know it or not. I've been studying some of the newer DNA data and am surprised and delighted by how many people don't realize some deep, dark family secret about some outlying branch of their family. Oh, the drama! Still, it's likely that your family is mostly from one area or another. If not, work with a couple of these suggested diets to figure out what's best for your body.

Chapter 6
How to Eat Like Your Ancestors

I hope that in the last chapter you were able to identify an area of the world that you can own as "your own," or perhaps you've picked two or three ancestral areas. It's okay if you have more than one; you can still figure out what works for your body and what doesn't work as well. This isn't a test and it isn't set in stone – it's more of a journey of foodie self-discovery.

If your ancestors were primarily from the **Mediterranean** countries including Turkey, Egypt, northern Africa, Spain, Italy, and southern France, then let's take a look at what your ancient family's daily diet might have looked like:

Breakfast
    Seasonal fruit like melon or figs, fresh soft goat cheese, and a little crusty bread.

Lunch
    A stew of eggplant, lamb, tomatoes, and plenty of herbs like oregano and rosemary, served over fresh pasta or couscous.

Dinner
    Calamari (squid) sautéed in butter and white wine and served with pine nuts. They might enjoy a couple of glasses of weak, low-alcohol or watered down wine.

~~~

In the more **northern parts of Europe, Scandinavia and the East European and western Russian states** their daily diet might have looked more like this:

Breakfast
    Hot porridge of oatmeal, barley, rye, cracked wheat, or even wild yellow dock seeds. This would be served with a good fat source like fresh cream or butter and perhaps some walnuts or other nuts. Chaga tea.

Lunch
    A liver or organ blend based sausage or "wurst" like Braunschweiger, liverwurst, or bratwurst served with hot cabbage and winter squash in the cold months, or sauerkraut and potato salad in the warm months. The potato salad is the kind made with lots of vinegar, which helps to digest the fats in the meal.

Inland Dinner

Roast game of any type, like boar (or pork), elk (or beef), pheasant (or chicken), and goose (or turkey). This might be served with root vegetables like rutabagas and turnips, and a hearty gravy cooked down and heavy-laden with savory herbs like tarragon, sage, and thyme. In the spring it would begin with a dandelion greens salad to help wake up the gall bladder from its long winter of cured, fatty meats, and summer and fall would include wild greens salads to initiate the meals.

Seaside Dinner

Halibut or flounder poached in butter and stock (bouillon); the sauce might be spiced and thickened with kelp (seaweed) and contain fresh picked raspberries. On the side you'd see a combination of onion, carrot, and potatoes boiled collectively, drained, and mashed together with cream or butter. Let's have a pint or two of microbrewery beer to help wash it down and unwind from the work day.

~~~

When we look at **South-East Asia** we think of vegetables and rice. This part of the world, including China, Japan, Burma/Myanmar, Vietnam, Thailand, Indonesia, and the other island and archipelago countries have very high-density urban areas where too many people are crammed into each square mile or kilometer. There is a large gap between the rich and poor, and the poorer people work very hard to get enough food, let alone enough protein. They eat a lot of rice because enough rice can be grown in a small plot of land to feed many, many families for a year.

This is where I'm going to digress and tell you a story about rice. Over a hundred years ago there was a drought in Southeast Asia and there wasn't enough rice grown that year to feed the people. A frightening percentage of the people died of starvation. This caused some of the countries to set up a protocol of saving a percentage of each year's rice crop to stave off any future shortages due to drought or other natural disaster. They quickly figured out that some rice would spoil or go rancid over time and that by "polishing" it (removing the outer hulls of the rice kernels) the rice would store much longer and they would have less loss. Sounds good, right?

Well, years went by and the people loved the taste of the white "polished" rice, probably because it had an almost double glycemic index and gave them a nice sugar high compared to brown "unpolished" rice. So white rice became the starch of choice.

Some number of years later there was an odd outbreak of disease symptoms that started out with weight loss and general muscle weakness and pain. Some people would regress into neurological degeneration that included the entire nervous system, neuropathy, paralysis, and difficulty speaking, eventually digressing into mental disease and death. Other patients would regress with heart and lung issues that had symptoms of increased heart beats, an enlarged heart, trouble breathing, and edema, eventually leading to heart failure and death. This disease was commonly called beriberi.

As the story goes, two doctors from two different parts of the world studied beriberi at the same time in the 1890s. They were Dr. Takaki Kanehiro from Japan and Dr. Christiaan Eijkman from the Netherlands. Neither of them ever met or knew about the other doctor, but they both came to the same conclusion: that beriberi was caused by a poor diet primarily consisting of white rice, and it could be easily remedied by adding a more varied and nutritious diet. By the way, Eijkman won the Nobel Prize for Physiology or Medicine in 1929 for his discovery.

And that's why I'm all about brown rice, red rice, black rice, wild rice, and any other type of unpolished rice you can get your hands on.

Where were we? Oh yeah, let's look at what we would be traditionally eating during a typical day in **South-East Asia.**

Breakfast
Starchy dumplings wrapped around a little spiced ground meat.
Hot green tea.

Lunch
Brown rice cooked in leftover fish broth with added sea greens (kelp or some other type of seaweed); let's go ahead and drop an egg into the soup while it's boiling.

Dinner
Soba noodles made from buckwheat flour topped with a fowl like duck or pheasant. There are plenty of spices and hot peppers in this part of the world, so don't hesitate to try them all out. They can really get your circulation going.

Let's add a big side of bok choy or other steamed or fermented vegetable in the cabbage family, as well as a little serving of rice wine of your choosing.

What's missing from the Asian diet? Milk and cheese. As a race, Asians are the most likely to be lactose intolerant, largely because their ancestors never drank milk past being weaned from their mothers. They simply didn't make or eat cheeses. Their bodies didn't need to produce lactase, the enzyme that helps digest lactose and other milk sugars. However, their diet does include pickled and fermented foods like kimchi, and the Japanese eat different pickled vegetables almost daily in their traditional diet.

~~~

Ah, **South and Central America**, where there are still many pockets where indigenous peoples live the same way that their ancestors lived centuries and millennia ago. They farm the steep mountains; herd sheep, goats, lamas, and alpacas; spin and weave wool; and hunt and gather. Those who choose to live this way have long, hearty lives. Those who move to the cities generally don't. We have a lot to learn from them both.

Breakfast

Scrambled eggs wrapped in freshly ground corn tortillas along with some of last night's leftover beans and vegetables. A small cup of nopal cactus fruit on the side. Let's have some black coffee with that.

Lunch

Catch of the day seafood steamed in plantain leaves and served with starchy yucca root. And we can have a beer with that, OK?

Dinner

Wild boar roasted all day in a pit of hot coals, served with a pot full of black beans and onions spiced with cilantro and lots of pepper. Una mas cervesa por favor!

~~~

Far north North Americans, as mentioned before, naturally have a very high fat diet due to the short flora growing season and the necessity of a rich diet to help survive the long cold winters.

Breakfast

Porridge cooked from seeds of various plants like burdock, yellow dock, or buckwheat. There are many different types of berries available in the boreal forests that can be added to the hot cereal. I'm not saying that you have to find and harvest these wild grains, but play around with a few of the ones that are more commonly found in grocery stores, like buckwheat and millet. Don't forget to put a dab of real maple syrup in your warm, comforting bowl of goodness.

Lunch

This meal might often be eaten on the road, so it might consist of dried meats like jerky, or roasted smaller animals including rabbit or fresh water fish. Vegetables might include carrots, peas, onions, squash, and corn, or a salad of sorts including watercress or wild carrot (Queen Anne's Lace) greens.

Dinner

Red meat roasted with the bones in to get all of the nutrients out of the bone and marrow. The choice organs like heart, liver, and sweetbread would go to the elders and pregnant women – those who need those densely nutritious portions the most. This could be served with baked grains, including wheat, buckwheat, and barley.

~~~

And now the **Middle East,** with all of those ancient grains, warm spices, and varied meats. The same foods that Moses, Jesus, the pharaohs, and sheiks ate. Lamb and goat, chicken and fowl, and some seafood for protein. A variety of grains such as couscous, millet, and bulgur as well as wonderful legumes including garbanzo beans/chickpeas (hummus) and lentils. Many types of fermented milks and cheeses, as well as some fermented vegetables. Just about every aromatic spice known to man is introduced into their foods, so please experiment, explore, and broaden your herbal horizons.

Breakfast

Manakeesh. Who doesn't love breakfast pizza? Well, they figured that out centuries ago in the Middle East, where manakeesh is a pizza shaped bread topped with cheese, a little ground meat, and lots of herbs.

Lunch

Falafel (your chickpeas again) filled with herbs and spices and served on a bed of fresh greens of your choice, dressed with a creamy oil, vinegar, and dill sauce.

Dinner

Shanklish salad to start, which is fresh cheese balls rolled in herbs and chili flakes, usually served with diced vegetables like onions and tomatoes. This can be followed by many types of spiced ground meats. This part of the world was civilized well before many others areas, as demonstrated by the long history of curing meats with salts and spices to prolong their shelf life as well as to augment their flavor. Again, please explore the many spiced meats and savories available from the cradle of civilization.

If your heritage is largely **Northern African,** then please look back to the cuisine suggestions for either the Mediterranean region or the Middle Eastern region. If your heritage is from **any of the balance of the African continent,** then your ancestors were blessed with rich rain forests, endless coastlines of oceans, bountiful rivers, vast mesas, and some of the most beautiful landscape in the world.

Breakfast
    Ugali (cornmeal) with eggs and chai tea. Beans and a tomato are always favorite side dishes.

Lunch
    Salad of collard greens and kale with a rounded helping of nicely spiced brown rice cooked in coconut milk.

Dinner

Hearty stew with a protein of your choosing simmered with some base vegetables like carrots, peas, or any type of pepper. The stew sauce is often tomato based. Let's have a side of green peas and potatoes boiled together and then mashed up with local herbs, or rice spiced with cumin, cardamom, cinnamon, and cloves to bring a fragrant tone to your meal.

All of these regional diets are squarely in the Paleo Diet arena and would be nourishing to most of you reading this book. Now, get shopping and get cooking!

Chapter 7
What to Drink

Whenever someone brags to me that they drink half their body weight in ounces of water each day I have to consciously refrain from rolling my eyes. Yes, fresh water is important, but did our ancestors really drink that much fresh water? Unless they were toiling outdoors in the fields during the hottest days of summer, no. Please understand; fresh water is a luxury. As true a luxury as electricity, automation, and chocolate.

Back in the day, people knew that standing water was unsafe to drink. It likely had insect larva and any number of pathogens and germs in it. If you were lucky enough to live near a quickly running brook, stream, creek, or river and you knew that there were no people or animals upstream from it bathing, washing, and doing other bodily functions in it, then you were truly blessed. Everyone else had to treat their water before they could drink it. With me so far?

With this in mind, what would you do? Well, if I had to boil my water before drinking it, I would probably give it some added value, like make a tea with it by adding any number of herbs to the water. I would go out in the woods or fields and gather plants that I recognized and wanted in my tea, either to make it taste better or to give it health benefits.

Another way to "treat" water is to ferment it. I could boil it with malted barley and add hops or some other bittering agent to make "wort" (beer before it has fermented), and then add yeast or let it ferment naturally to make farmhouse ale. Wine is another way to ferment grapes in water and make it safe to drink. I had a roommate from Germany and she told me her middle and high school served "light" beer to the students in the 1980s because the local water wasn't safe. I have a feeling that this is still true today.

People tend to forget that many freshly picked fruits and vegetables have a lot of water in them inherently. Soups, stews, and sauces have liquid in them, but they can't have too much salt, which would negate the action. If you're eating these types of foods, then you're getting liquids that can be counted toward your water intake.

Now let's turn this idea around.

Do you think someone can drink too much water? When I was going to college in St. Louis, Missouri, there was a big brouhaha about a local radio station that gave away a car to the person who could drink the most water. Each contestant signed a legal waiver, of course, but it went bad quickly. The woman who won drank so much water that her kidneys shut down, she was rushed to the hospital, and she died. She died. From drinking too much water. It makes me wonder if some people who drink so much water on a daily basis might be harming their kidneys.

And then there are the dozens of theories about what kind of water is the best: should you should drink filtered, tap, city, country, well, reverse osmosis, bottled, etc., etc., etc. How about this: Just drink water. There are way too many other things to worry about to spend that much time worrying about what kind of water to drink. Personally, I worry a whole lot about how many millions of empty water bottles are discarded into landfills every single day. I also worry about the toxins that are released during the manufacturing process for said bottles, and filling them, and transporting them to the store.

Drink less water, take it out of the tap, and if you live in a typical city that puts literally 150+ chemicals in their drinking water, well then, filter it before drinking it. You can go to your city or township office and ask for a report on the water. By law they have to have it tested by an outside source at least once a year. That report should also have a list of the chemicals that they put into the water system. I'm very lucky, as the public water in my small town only adds chlorine, and then only when needed. Please don't ask me about fluoride, as that answer is for another book.

And please, stop buying bottled water. Instead, buy a metal or glass container to put your own water into. You'll save money and the Earth at the same time.

What do I do for myself? When I first wake up in the morning I drink an eight-ounce glass of water. I've been sleeping a long while, and perhaps snoring or at least had my mouth gaping open for a while. I'm thirsty, so I drink water. After that I drink a cup or two of different types of teas. I don't like coffee myself, but I don't have anything against it as long as it is a cup or two a day. An eight ounce cup of coffee, not a mug half the size of a pot of coffee.

Then there's breakfast, after which I let my stomach digest and rest before lunch. There's a difference between an "empty" stomach and a "hungry" stomach, so it's OK if my stomach is empty for a while before lunch. Besides, I have things to do.

When I eat lunch I don't drink anything with it. I am a firm believer that drinking any liquid with a meal dilutes the stomach acids and they can't work as well. Lunch and dinner is focused on the food, ignoring the drink. When I combine the two there is a chance that I could have some indigestion, which I never seem to suffer from when I just eat food without the beverage. Try it out and see if you feel differently.

The afternoon is spent working or playing and if I get hungry I have a cup of low-caffeine or herbal tea. If I'm thirsty I have a glass of water. Then I get back to work/play.

Dinner is dinner, again without liquids. Sure, I'll have a beer or glass of wine before dinner, and sometimes after dinner. Many times I'll have a glass sitting at the table while eating, but you won't see me drinking out of it very often.

If you're one of those adults that like milk and it agrees with them, let's have the rest of "the milk conversation" here. We humans used to drink raw milk. Unfortunately, there were (and are still) many areas of milk production that have the possibility of contamination. Many, many people used to die from drinking milk that was contaminated, had any number of pathogens, or was spoiled. So we figured out that if we pasteurized it, in essence heated it, it would kill the nasty little critters and make it safe to drink. Although many people are big fans of raw milk, my personal take is that pasteurization simply prevents unnecessary sickness and death, so I strongly suggest drinking pasteurized milk.

I'm much more concerned about the amount of fat in the milk that you're drinking. Yes, fat is high in calories – nine calories per gram. Sugar is only four calories per gram. Protein is only four calories per gram. Even with this in mind, I prefer the highest fat content milk available. Why? Here's a list:

- The higher the fat content, the higher the satiety (the longer you feel full).
- The higher the fat content, the longer the shelf life.
- The higher the fat content, the lower the sugar (lactose) content.
- The higher the fat content, the less processed it is.

My family doesn't drink milk, but I keep a pint of half-and-half in my 'fridge for cooking purposes. Oh, and for the occasional hot chocolate in the winter time.

Chapter 8
Frequently Asked Questions

"What about milk?" As my dear husband has said countless times, "Humans are the only mammals that don't wean their young." He is lactose intolerant, as are so many adults. Let's think historically here; the first man to drink milk from a cow/goat/camel/etc. must have been really desperate, right? Why do I say "he"? Because it was most likely a new father whose wife just died in childbirth and he needed to feed their newborn. In this case I can easily see desperation leading to ingenuity.

But at some point in time and in many parts of the world the children were never weaned.

Yes, I am saying that milk should not be drunk by most adults. I do, however, use it in moderation in my cooking, and I do eat small quantities of cheese. In my experience in the nutrition field I find that many Europeans do just fine drinking milk, but that those of Asian and African heritage are more likely to be lactose intolerant.

"What about cheese?" In my experience, again, people have fewer gastrointestinal problems with softer cheeses than harder cheeses. So if you're lactose intolerant and want to dip your toe into the pool of dairy I suggest starting out with yogurt to see how it might affect you. If you don't have problems with that I suggest next trying cottage cheese, then feta or goat's cheese, or maybe brie. I do not suggest jumping on the cheddar bandwagon, as those good hard "brick" cheeses seem to render the worst effects.

"You're not going to take away my ice cream, are you?" Um, yes. OK, I have ice cream twice a year: once at my granddaughter's birthday and once at my grandson's birthday. There is absolutely nothing natural about humans eating ice cream. Or dogs. I know way too many people who feed their pets ice cream. These pets age much faster and tend to get specific health problems, including joint problems and "fatty cysts." Please stop feeding your pets sweets and highly processed treats; it's literally killing them with kindness.

"I live in the city and have no interest in hunting. What do I do?" Yeah, that's a good question and I've been thinking about it while writing this book. Please understand that I don't enjoy cities. Too many people, too much noise, and considerably too much stimulation. But I also realize that some people thrive on it. It might make living a Paleo life more expensive unless you get crafty. "City people" can still have a small freezer along with your refrigerator to keep bulk-bought beef, buffalo, wild fowl, and fish. You can still frequent farmer's markets for at least half of the year, depending on how close to the equator you live. You can still have a well-stocked pantry, learn half a dozen recipes from scratch, and learn to use left-overs. The more I think about it the more I realize that being a non-hunter in the city is no different than being a non-hunter in the suburbs or the country.

"I live alone and it's not prudent for me to buy bulk foods." It can be more expensive to shop and cook for one, I understand. Remember the old adage "Two can live as cheaply as one"? Two things I can suggest for you: don't buy too much food, and use left-overs.

Not buying too much food also means that you'll probably be buying smaller amounts of food every day or every other day. Actually, that's a great way to go anyway. It doesn't mean that you have to spend hours each day at the store on your way home from work; find a smaller store with their fresh produce just inside the door and near the check-out area.

Left-overs are wonderful, embrace them. Most foods are better the next day because the herbs and spices have had more time to be instilled into the victuals. I've known a number of busy single people who prepare all of their lunches and dinners for the week on Sunday.

"We are retired and living on a budget and we can't get out like we used to." Cool! That means that you're probably old enough to know how to cook and follow recipes! Choose five or more recipes for each season and switch them up throughout the year. Find a soup, stew, roast, and a couple of other favorites for springtime with early green leafy vegetables and seafood or perhaps some lamb. Pick five or more for fresh summer meals and add some grilled foods, find five more for fall's bounty of root vegetables and squashes and late season fruits like grapes and apricots, and five more hearty meals to get you through the cold short winter days. There are countless "seasonal" cook books to help you on this journey.

"I just hate chopping up foods and even cooking. Can't I get those things in grocery stores?" The first thing that pops into my mind is "Grow up!" OK, that's not fair. I know that we all have our talents and many are not talented at food preparation. Go ahead and buy restaurant and grocery prepared foods, just make sure that they don't have added ingredients and preservatives. Read all labels. For instance, that "rotisserie chicken" sitting out in a warming kiosk at the grocery store is literally injected with up to 20 chemicals to enhance flavor and make it safe for it to sit out for so many hours. Another "for instance" is that most restaurant salad bars spray the fresh lettuces and greens with a chemical preservative that is widely known to cause toxic symptoms in people who eat at salad bars too often. Ask questions at restaurants, and search out restaurants that are not chains, but rather are owned by a family where they make all of their foods from scratch in-house.

"I only eat out, what should I order in restaurants?" Alright, here is a list of things commonly found in sit-down restaurants. Of course, food establishments that make their food from scratch are best, and keep in mind that many restaurants just open pre-prepared foods in plastic pouches purchased from Costco and Gordon Food Service, heat them up, and put them on a plate before bringing it to your table, so there might be a little homework involved to find out which places have the freshest foods. Some key tag lines for fresher, made-from-scratch establishments are "farm to table," "sourced locally," and "made fresh daily."

- A salad without croutons and with steak, shrimp, hard boiled eggs, or chicken. Don't go to a help-yourself salad bar too often because they spray the greens with a preservative to prevent them from wilting. People have become toxic on this spray when eaten too often.

- Any type of meat that is baked or broiled, like roast beef, turkey, chicken, or planked fish.

- Whole meats. Think about it this way: picture a leg of beef hanging at the butcher. They cut a roast off of it, and that's still "whole." They can take the roast and slice it into many steaks and it's still considered "whole." They can take the steaks and grind it up into hamburger or sausage, and at this point I don't consider it "whole." Why? Because there is too much surface area where oxygen can penetrate it, make it rancid, and possibly contaminate any surface. The less oxidation and less chance of spoilage and rancidity the better, right? In short, the less cut up it is the more "whole."

- Skip the potatoes, especially if you can't control yourself around them like me. I just order with vegetables only because I know that I'll end up scarfing down all of the spuds. A few bites are alright though.

- Eat mushrooms, all different kinds of edible mushrooms. Button, portabella, enoki, shiitake, chanterelle, morel. They are healthy beyond imagining and are clinically proven to modulate the immune system. There are more than one hundred published peer-reviewed clinical trials showing a connection to mushrooms and many forms of cancer. Simply put, people who eat more mushrooms or take mushroom extract supplements are shown to have significantly less rates of cancer and types of cancer.

- Order clear soups, not creamy soups. For instance, Manhattan clam chowder with a clear broth, tomatoes and beans, instead of Boston clam chowder made with cream and thickening agents like wheat flour or agar.

- If you can afford it, eat good cuts of steak. Keep in mind that many cuts are seasoned and/or "tenderized" with chemicals and salts, like beef brisket and prime rib. Stick to a plain old fashioned steak.

- Sea food, as in "from the sea," where they are chock-full of all of the 70-plus minerals that our bodies need. Fresh water fish are good, don't get me wrong, and although they can give you a good dose of healthy fats and proteins, they don't have the inherent minerals that salt water seafood does. My favorites are halibut, salmon, sea bass, muscles, and squid. Squid is especially wonderful when it's not covered in breading and deep fried. The United States is the only country in the world whose citizens don't regularly consume squid or sea vegetables like dulse and nori, for that matter. When buying and eating shellfish like shrimp, crab, lobster, and crawfish, try to make sure that they are wild-caught and not farm-raised. Farm-raised seafood doesn't contain as many of those all-important minerals.

- Branch out from the "normal" vegetables and experiment with some that you perhaps haven't had before. I'm a big proponent of a variable diet because you need a variety of foods to get a variety of nutrients. Try some of these:

- Root vegetables: Beets (don't forget the greens!), Jerusalem artichokes, parsnips, yams, turnips, rutabagas, and leeks.
- Greens: spinach, beet greens, bok choy greens, mustard greens and garlic mustard greens, endive, kale, collard greens, chard, parsley, turnip greens, and watercress.
- Above ground vegetables: Asparagus, cucumbers, endive, escarole, radishes, summer and winter squashes, peppers of all kinds, okra, artichokes, avocados, Brussels sprouts, and jicama.
- Legumes: Step away from baked beans and really enjoy black beans, pigeon peas (black eyed peas), chickpeas (garbanzo beans), different types of lentils, split peas, many kidney beans, or (gasp) a 15 bean blend!
- Grains: There is a world of grains out there besides wheat. Have you tried quinoa, buckwheat, steel cut oats, amaranth, barley, red rice, wild rice, or millet?
- Fermented foods: try other pickled vegetables beyond cucumbers, sauerkraut, yogurt, and kefir (liquid yogurt).

Every continent has their fermented favorites, so do a little homework and find out what your ancestors savored.
- Healthy vegetable oils: coconut oil, macadamia nut oil, sesame oil, and good old olive oil. Avocado oil is my new favorite, as it can be heated to very high temperatures without smoking or chemically changing. There are whole isles of healthy oils in larger grocery stores today. Experiment.
- Sprouts: Yes these were quite the fad in the 1970s and 1980s, but they really are good for you. Pick up a package the next time you're at the grocery store and add them to a salad, sandwich, or hamburger. You might be surprised at how many varieties your local grocer has in stock.

- Herbs. Really, herbs are super foods, and the minute you decide to set aside the salt and pepper and use fresh or dried herbs instead is the minute you've made up your mind to be healthier. To help you out here is a snippet of herb-food pairings.

- Tarragon is always a welcome addition to any bird or fowl recipe. Add it by the tablespoon (no pinches here) to baked chicken, duck, turkey, guinea hen, pheasant, or goose.
- A couple of bay leaves can be placed on top of any type of roast to add sweetness without sugar. It can be added to soups, stews, and chili for the same reason. Make sure to remove them before eating though, or else you'll be chewing on some pretty indigestible leaves.
- Dill is wonderful sprinkled on any type of fish, or in a sauce to spread on top or dip it into. An easy fish recipe is to put some thawed mild fish like cod or sole in the center of a sheet of aluminum foil. Bring up the edges of the foil to make a bowl. Sprinkle plenty of dill and some white pepper on top, squeeze some lemon juice, ¼ cup finely chopped onion, and ¼ cup salsa. Bring the edges of the foil up and seal the contents inside. Place in a large frying pan or on the grill for about 10 minutes. When the fish is opaque white in the middle after lifting a flake up it is done. If it's still translucent

(clear) it's not quite done and you should give it a couple more minutes in the pan.

"What is a healthy diet?" If you follow the information provided in this book, it would be a moderation of real, fresh, clean foods and beverages.

Chapter 9
Moderation, My Friends

By now you're probably thinking, "This woman is great! She says I can eat all the meat that I want!" And if that's what you're thinking, then I'm here to rein you in a little. Or a lot.

Depending on your height and your activity level you really don't need that much meat protein in your diet. If you are overweight at all you don't need that much *food* in your diet. Here are some examples, and remember that these are my opinions based on results from my clients:

- If you are of average height (between 5'6" and 6"0") and have a job where you get an average amount of exercise every day (waiter/waitress, cook, grocery stocker) you probably only need 4 to 8 oz. of animal protein a day. That's a small steak the size of the palm of your hand plus an egg.
    - If you have a desk job, then you need less than this amount of protein and a lot fewer calories. You probably don't need more than 2,000 calories a day and can live a healthy life when including only 3 oz. to 6 oz. of protein per day.
    - If you are an athlete, lumberjack, construction worker, or have some similar high-caloric-output profession, then you need a lot more protein and food in general. You could be expending more than 4,000 calories a day. You may need up to 8 oz. of protein per day.
    - The rest of your daily food menus should be filled with a variety of raw and lightly cooked colorful vegetables, a few root vegetables and fresh fruits, some unmilled grains, rice, and legumes, and very little milled flours.

- If you are petite or diminutive (below 5'6") and get an average amount of exercise every day, then you probably only need 3 oz. to 6 oz. of animal protein a day. To give you proper perspective, a half-pound hamburger is 8 oz. You may adjust this as above for more or less daily activity, and be honest with yourself about your calorie output.

- If you are tall (as in over 6'0") then you likely need more protein and calories in general than someone shorter, but I warn you again to be honest about the amount of exercise that you get. If you're too heavy, then figure out what foods you can cut out, and start with breads and pastas.

This all reminds me of a story about what happened after one of my best friends got married. My friend is 5'4" tall and her then new husband was a good 6'2" tall. She is a little competitive. Okay, a lot competitive, and she naturally ate as much as he did. It took her about two years to figure out why she had gained so much weight and then it took a few more months for her to wrap her mind around the challenge of reining in her competitive tendencies so that she could begin eating and drinking considerably less than her dear husband.

"But it's not fair!" she wailed at me one day.

"Of course it's not." I said as I gave her a supportive hug.

I want you to do something for me: take one of your hands and make a fist. Now make it into a loose fist, not so tight. Hold it in front of where your stomach is, between the bottom two points of your ribcage. That is the size of your stomach.

Let me say it again, *that* is the size of your stomach.

Do you eat more than that volume at one meal? What would happen if you only ate that much food at one meal?

In my experience it takes no more than 10 days to shrink your stomach back down to its original normal size and once this is done many food cravings subside. I know one man who lost more than 20 pounds and kept it off by traveling around with a coffee mug about the size of his fist. He was a traveling salesman and he realized that his excess weight was caused by eating too much food, mostly in restaurants, and by his hours and hours of sitting behind the wheel of a car. Once his stomach was shrunk back down he trained himself on how to order food and how much to leave on his plate.

We people in the "First World" who have too much food and not enough physical work are too often addicted to putting things into our mouths. Are you addicted to putting food in your mouth? And if it's not food, then a beverage, or cough drop, a pen or pencil to your mouth, or a cigarette? Do you pick at your lips or fondle your chin? How much more productive would you be if you simply stopped putting your hand to your mouth? How much better would you feel if you broke your addiction to thinking about feeding your mouth most of your waking hours?

It is clinically proven that people who are overweight due to a low-protein, high-carbohydrate diet are more likely to contract diabetes, heart disease, and other sugar related diseases.

It is clinically proven that people who are overweight due to a high-protein and high-fat diet are prone to diseases of the heart including arteriolosclerosis (hardening of the arteries), unbalanced cholesterol, and vascular maladies like varicose veins and hemorrhoids.

It is clinically proven that people who eat in moderation, exercise in moderation, drink alcohol, tea, and water in moderation, work and play in moderation, are more likely to live long, comfortable lives. It may sound boring, but a life filled with balance is, in my not-so-humble opinion, the way to go.

Chapter 10
Find Your Meatatarian Way

I do understand why so many people are against slaughter-houses and factory farms. I truly do. I am blessed to know a local small farmer who always has a cow or two happily grazing in his side lot and occasionally I split one of his non-certified-organic but still quite organic bovines with some friends.

What else can you do to eat better without going broke or having to spend too much time cooking? I offer my experience as proof that you can eat the Meatatarian Way, too. This is what it looks like in real life:

- We have a small garden that my father and I tend in the summer that gives us potatoes, peas, beans, and other goodies. Okay, my father does most of the work, along with his good friend Herk. My dear husband grows hops there, too, for home brewing.

- I bought a book or two on charcuterie and have learned to make my own bacon. I truly hate sulfites and I truly love bacon. So, it seemed like the wisest thing to do. It also taught me how to cure meats, sausages, and pâtés, which I like to work on a few Saturday afternoons per year. It works for me; it might not work for you.

- I buy large quantities of our favorite vegetables from the farmers market every summer and can (pressure cook) them.

It's hot, it takes a whole day a few Saturdays per summer, but it feeds us all winter and I believe it's worth it. You don't have to do it.

I encourage you to do your best to eat healthy, especially if (like me) you have had an "a-ha moment" of realization that health is closely related to what we eat. It took me decades to get to this point. I also realize that my personal diet menu will be a work in progress for the remainder of my life. I certainly don't have it all figured out, and I don't expect that I ever will. I still buy food from the grocery store way too often because I work too many hours a week, have parents, a spouse, kids, and grandkids, and too many projects to mention. Who has time to eat perfectly? Nobody. Forgive yourself. You are doing your best and it's a work in progress.

Forgive yourself and do your best.

Now, get online and search for foods and recipes from your ancestral area of the world, and write down a shopping list, and get cooking. I hope you thoroughly enjoy your journey of ancestral foodie discoveries!

References

Cordain, L., Miller, J.B., Eaton, S.B., Mann, N., Holt, S.H., & Speth, J.D. (2000 Mar). Plant-animal subsistence ratios and macronutrient energy estimations in worldwide hunter-gatherer diets. *American Journal of Clinical Nutrition,* 71(3), 682-92. Retrieved from https://www.ncbi.nlm.nih.gov/pubmed/10702160

Gillen, J. (2008). Obligate Carnivore: Cats, Dogs & What it Really Means to be Vegan. Charleston, South Carolina: BookSurge Publishing.

Haas, E. (2006). Staying Healthy with Nutrition. Berkeley, CA: Celestial Arts Publishing.

Made in the USA
Middletown, DE
07 March 2018